MOBILISATION AND MANAGEMENT

A STUDY IN THE LIFE OF MOSES (Numbers 11)

By

CATHERINE BROWN

Published by
The Transparent Publishing Company

www.TransparentPublishing.co.uk

Paperback ISBN 9781909805194

eBook ISBN 9780956208668

First published March 2012
Original Copyright holder - Catherine Brown

Cover Photography by Peter Ribbeck
www.PeterRibbeck.com

Unless otherwise stated all Scriptures quoted
are from New International Version

MOBILISATION AND MANAGEMENT

- A STUDY IN THE LIFE OF MOSES

CONTENTS

MOBILISATION AND MANAGEMENT

- A STUDY IN THE LIFE OF MOSES

CHAPTER 1: FIRST STEPS

Wherever Jesus ministered, His presence drew crowds and gathered multitudes to the Father leading to multi-faceted expressions of the Kingdom being manifested on the earth. From this Biblical blueprint we comprehend that the apostolic anointing has an ability to gather. Gathering has the effect of building momentum, which becomes a catalyst under the anointing of God's Holy Spirit to cause mobilisation that leads to acceleration, multiplication and advancement of God's Kingdom on earth. Hallelujah!

I believe we are in a season of global outpouring of apostolic grace on the church to enable the church fulfil the Great Commission. As more and more believers respond to the harvest mandate, there will be worldwide mobilisation of the church for the glory of God. Whilst this is a wonderful spiritual reality, we must also embrace the more sobering and perhaps difficult aspects of mobilisation, in that there are many potential pitfalls ahead.

The following short study from the life of Moses, will give both the servant "leader" and the "follower" spiritual "food for thought," which I hope will prove to be a Godly plumb-line, blessing and an encouragement to all.

Management of people is not an easy task; in truth mobilisation often causes complaining, fault finding, carnality, attack on leaders and downright rebellion against God. In this article we will look at the effects of **complaining, craving** and **compromise** by studying three different incidents in Moses' life during the time when the Israelites were being mobilised by the Lord.

MOSES – A THUMBNAIL SKETCH OF HIS LIFE

- Moses – Levite – brother of Aaron (ex 6:20, 1 Ch 6:3)
- Put in a basket in the Nile; discovered and raised by Pharaoh's daughter (Ex 2:1-10)
- Fled to Midian after killing an Egyptian (Ex 2:11-15)
- Married Zipporah and fathered Gershom (Ex 2:16-22)
- Called by the Lord to deliver Israel (Ex 3, 4)
- Pharaoh's resistance (Ex 5)
- Ten plagues (Ex 7-11)
- Passover and Exodus (Ex 12-13)
- Led Israel through the Red Sea (Ex 14)
- Song of deliverance (Ex 15:1-21)
- Brought water from the rock (Ex 17:1-7)

- Raised hands to defeat Amalakites (Ex 17:8-16)
- Delegated Judges (Ex 18, Dt 1:9-18)
- Received Law at Sinai (Ex 19-23; 25-31; Jn 1:17)
- Broke tablets due to the golden calf and Israel's idolatry (Ex 32; Dt 9)
- Saw the glory of the Lord (Ex 33, 34)
- Set apart Aaron and priest (Lev 8-9)
- Opposed by Aaron and Miriam (Nu 12)
- Sent spies into Canaan (Nu 13)
- Announced 40 years of wandering for failure to enter land (Nu 16)
- Opposed by Korah (Nu 16)
- Forbidden to enter land for striking rock (Nu 20:1-13, Dt 1:37)
- Lifted bronze snake for healing (Nu 21:4-9; Jn 3:14)
- Succeeded by Joshua (Nu 27:12-23; Dt 34)
- Death (Dt 34:5-12)
- "Law of Moses" (1 Ki 2:3; Ezr 3:2; Mk 12:26; Lk 24:44)
- "Book of Moses" (2 Ch 25:12; Ne 13:1)
- "Song of Moses" (Ex 15:1-21; Rev 15:3)
- "Prayer of Moses" (Ps 90)

MOSES AND THE ISRAELITES

"Whether the cloud stayed over the tabernacle for two days or a month or a year, the Israelites would remain in camp and not set out; but when

it lifted they would set out. At the Lord's command they encamped, and at the Lord's command they set out. They obeyed the Lord's order, in accordance with his command through Moses." Numbers 9:22-23

On the day the tabernacle was set up, the cloud of God rested above it and it looked like fire. The people of God would set out whenever the cloud lifted at the Lord's command (which they received through his anointed leader Moses) and they would settle again whenever and wherever the cloud settled. Sometimes this was only for a day, at other times it could rest in one place for a whole year but whatever length of time the cloud remained the Israelites encamped or set out in obedience to the command of the Lord.

The Israelites waited for the Lord's signal before they moved out in mobilisation. They trusted the protection of His presence, evidenced by the holy fire above the tabernacle. Likewise, today it is essential that we are led by the Holy Spirit into the new things of God. A people of God's presence will become a people entrusted with God's power, so long as we remain humble and obedient before Him.

The Israelites were in covenant relationship with God and were being established in His purposes and plans. God was developing strong spiritual foundations in them through their leader Moses.

Leaders have the humble privilege of helping to establish strong faith foundations in others.

To be established in God's presence means we have a secure covenant relationship with the Lord that enables us to respond in radical obedience to move into God's purposes for our lives. Such foundations enable us to become resolute in pursuing and embracing God's purposes and plans as we wholly surrender our lives to His will

LED BY THE SPIRIT

The tribes of Israel moved out in a divinely mandated order as the divisions of the camp set out one-by-one. The Ark of the Covenant of God went before them and the cloud of the Lord was over them by day (Numbers 10, 15-23, + v33, 34) The Israelites also responded to trumpet blasts on silver trumpets blown by Aaron's sons, who were the priests. These gave different instructions such as gathering of the heads of the clans, gathering for assembly at the Tent of Meeting and setting out of the tribes. The Israelites were also reminded to blow the trumpets in times of rejoicing, such as the New Moon festivals as a memorial before the Lord.

The Bible teaches us as New Testament believers that "*Since we live by the Spirit, let us keep in step with the Spirit.*" (Galatians 5:25)

God also spoke to the Israelites,

"When you go into battle in your own land against an enemy who is oppressing you, sound a blast on the trumpets. Then you will be remembered by the Lord your God and rescued from your enemies." Numbers 10:9

When the people set out with the Ark of the Covenant Moses prayed,

"Rise up, O Lord! May your enemies be scattered! May your foes flee before you." Whenever the cloud came to rest he would pray, "Return, O Lord, to the countless thousands of Israel." (Numbers 10:35)

Penetrating new territory is part of pioneering, which in turn is an element of mobilisation. Such pioneering activity will often involve head on encounter with enemy opposition. So whether one is at the forefront of leading or following in the footsteps of a servant leader, this is an excellent prayer for every believer involved in mobilising! Not only did Moses pray for God to arise and scatter his enemies, but Moses was also careful to pray for the Lord's presence to return to the multitudes of Israel.

SHIFT INTO APOSTOLIC PARADIGM

"As they were setting out Moses spoke to Hobab and encouraged him to come with them saying, "Please do not leave us. You know where we should camp in the desert, and you can be our eyes." Numbers 10:31

Following on from Moses' request, it evident that he felt Hobab possessed some reconnaissance skills and had experience of the desert. Perhaps we might liken Hobab to one with "eyes to see" in terms of prophetic insight and interpretation. Moses was an apostolic leader and he chose to welcome the prophetic gift into the camp. **Apostolic grace, wisdom and prophetic insight are a powerful combination of gifting in the Lord.**

It is time for the global church to shift into the apostolic paradigm. A paradigm is simply a pattern or a model; in this context it simply means a way to "be" church and receive Christ's apostolic grace anointing by faith and walk in the blessing of fruitfulness that it releases to the church. Apostolic grace brings acceleration to the purposes and plans of God. It releases encouragement to and through the church.

The shift into apostolic paradigm makes room for all the gifts; apostolic and prophetic ministers lay strong foundations upon which the church can mature and enter into the fullness of God's blessing.

MOBILISATION AND MANAGEMENT

- A STUDY IN THE LIFE OF MOSES

CHAPTER 2: COMPLAINING

COMPLAINING IN THE CAMP

"Now the people complained about their hardships in the hearing of the Lord and when he heard them his anger was aroused. Then fire from the Lord burned among them and consumed some of the outskirts of the camp. When the people cried out to Moses, he prayed to the Lord and the fire died down. So that place was called Taberah, because fire from the Lord had burned among them." Numbers 11:1-3

The place where the fire burned in the camp was named *Taberah (*which means 'burning'). God was merciful to only burn the outskirts of the camp AND NOT THE PEOPLE, nonetheless His fire burned amongst His people. The fire was a visible sign of the manifest power and presence of God who was not willing to leave His children in the condition in which He found them, but was committed to journeying with them to remove the unlovely from their hearts. God is still sending the fire of His presence to conform our lives to His image!

Complaining is like spiritual dross that God burns away from the outskirts of our hearts

by sending the fire of His Holy Spirit. Just like the Israelites, when our routines are disturbed and we are moved from our "comfort zone" – whether literally or figuratively - we often resort to complaining before God. Often when we experience physical, emotional, mental or spiritual discomfort we complain; **God's grace is sufficient in such times to meet us in weakness and carry us through to victory in Him.**

In his second letter to the church in Corinth, Apostle Paul permits us to take a behind-the-scenes look at a part of his life that most leaders today would hesitate to share openly about – an aspect of personal suffering that he describes as a "*messenger of Satan*"! (2 Corinthians 12:7b). Can you imagine a pastor or ministry leader declaring to their flock that God had sent a messenger of Satan to them and then can you think about how the church might respond?! **Paul's forthrightness and transparency is testament to his humility and security in the Lord. May we take note of such character strength that flows from trusting in God with our lives.** May we also seek to emulate the level of agape in which Paul ministered.

Furthermore, Paul could have spoke to the Corinthians and pointed out *their faults*, but instead he chose a meeker posture and pointed to some of *his own struggles*. Paul had a "*thorn in his flesh,*" which he does not give specific details about other than he asked God to take it from him on three separate occasions. It doesn't take too big a stretch of the imagination to consider that just maybe, St Paul complained about that pain to God until he received understanding from God of the purpose of his trial. He describes it to us thus,

"To keep me from becoming conceited because of these surpassingly great revelations." (v7a) **By prayerfully seeking God in the midst of his life-trial Paul had gained divine perspective on his suffering, which caused him to rise above 'complaining' to soar on the wings of grace.**

God did not take away Paul's thorn; instead God gave Paul more grace:

"My grace is sufficient for you, for my power is made perfect in weakness. Therefore I will boast all the more gladly about my weaknesses, so that Christ's power may rest on me." 2 Corinthians 12:9

Today, we desperately need to understand and embrace the truth that God give us grace for the process of moving into the new things He has planned for us in our calling and destiny. Furthermore, grace is the means by which we maintain our faith responses through times of trial and testing as we rejoice in the Biblical truth that God rewards those who diligently seek Him. Hallelujah! (see Hebrews 11:6)

APOSTOLIC LEADERSHIP INTERVENTION = GAP STANDING

Moses prayed for his people and the fire died down. As Godly leaders we are called to love those with whom we co-labour and to intercede on behalf of those who complain. We all must come to the realisation that it is only by grace that the 'complainant' becomes compliant to God's will. We can learn from Apostle Paul that divinely decreed "weakness" is a position we are mandated for before God.

A surrendered heart is a perfect crucible through which God can manifest His holy power. Leadership is not about lording it over people, it is about loving people, helping others through issues, offering wisdom and remaining prayerful and diligent about releasing God's destiny in those whom we are blessed to oversee. We learn patience when we are compelled by God's love to walk with others through life issues. **Patience is developed in the valley of trial: our character is important as a lifestyle model to those whom we are entrusted to lead.**

CRAVINGS IN THE CAMP

"the rabble with them began to crave other foods and again Israel started wailing." Numbers 11:4

Most leaders will understand all too well that where there is a gathering of God's people, somewhere in the midst, there is often a "rabble." A rabble can be as few as one person or several. **It only takes one person who is discontented to negatively affect a whole group and the discord they sow can spread as fast as a viral airborne infection!** In this case the "rabble" was complaining about what they were being 'forced' to eat.

The people of Israel had left Egypt, where they once had access to fresh fish, melons, leeks, cucumbers, onion and garlic. Now they existed on manna that tasted a bit like coriander, that they had to grind and make into cakes. They were fed up with their diet and said,

"But now we have lost our appetite; we never see anything but this manna." Numbers 11:6

The Israelites craved meat. **They had a longing in their appetite that was contrary to what God had planned for that stage of their walk with Him. Apostle Paul teaches us in his letter to the church at Galatia that the carnal desires of our flesh will lead to destruction, whilst our walking by the Spirit leads to the blessing of eternal life.** Cravings of the flesh can lead to distractions/loss of focus; delay of blessings and ultimately destruction of destiny. The sad fact is that we often want things that are not good for us; God, on the other hand, is in the business of encouraging His children to have a "carnal free" diet.

"Do not be deceived: God cannot be mocked. A man reaps what he sows. The one who sows to please his sinful nature, from that nature will reap destruction; the one who sows to please the Spirit, from the Spirit will reap eternal life." Galatians 6:7-8

Often during mobilisation of new vision there is a "rabble" somewhere in the group of saints who have been gathered. This might be just one person with a difficult attitude, someone who is fearful or a person with their own 'agenda' (e.g. a desire for power). Such a person(s) has the potential to sow discord, division and disunity amongst God's people. A Godly leader must deal with such discord with decisive prayerful action, wisdom, and compassion.

*"Leading people is not just about plans, programs, and projects. Leading people is about developing their issues, ideas, advices, opinions to make meaning applicable and adoptable to their situations though diverse they may seem. **Not all the disagreements are unhealthy but scrutinized properly wells; treasures of jewels can be obtained**. Thus we do not lead people but lives full of issues, questions awaiting*

answers, joy awaiting expressions, tears wiggling in the eyes waiting to be shed. A successful leader is one who is able to produce himself/ herself in others." Apostle Edward Mbuyi, Uganda

Apostle Edward's insights give us a further perspective on complaining and help us to comprehend that a certain amount of conflict can produce good fruit when managed with wisdom and Godly insight. Nonetheless, we recognise that the discord that Moses' was dealing with had a different emphasis. Find out in chapter three how Moses dealt with the "rabble"!

MOBILISATION AND MANAGEMENT

- A STUDY IN THE LIFE OF MOSES

CHAPTER 3: 'CRAVINGS'

In Chapter 2 of our study we discussed the 'rabble' that had arisen during the mobilisation of God's people under Moses' leadership. We now turn our attention to Moses and ponder his responses during such a difficult transition.

Moses literally heard the people of every family wailing about the situation (v10). Like Moses, leaders today must have an ear to hear what is happening with their people. Part of being a responsible leader is to embrace the need to be prayerfully responsive when crisis occurs in the lives of those whom we lead. Prayerful response to such crises will, in turn, enable us to act with wisdom and compassion both for the individual and for the corporate body of believers.

MOSES FEELS THE BURDEN!

He asked the Lord, "*Why have you brought this trouble on your servant? What have I done to displease you that you put the burden of all these people on me? "Did I conceive all these people? Did I give them birth? Why do you tell me to carry them in my arms, as a nurse carries an infant to the land you promised on oath to their forefathers? Where can I get meat for all these people?"* v11-13

APOSTOLIC LEADERSHIP INTERVENTION = GAP STANDING IN PRAYER

Speaking frankly, Moses was probably ready for pulling his hair out! His words reflect the reality of the depth of his burden-bearing and frustration. At this point there are around 600,000 men on foot in the camp – that's excluding women and children. It is an enormous burden for Moses to bear and he has reached the end of his tether. It has been my experience that **every leader will come to this place of desperation before the Lord in managing people and there is only one safe place to go – to the Lord of Hosts in prayer, fellowship and deep communion, depending on His strength alone and in His wisdom and grace to deliver and lead our flocks/partners/team members.**

WISDOM IS KNOWING OUR LIMITATIONS AND TRUSTING OUR LIMITLESS GOD FOR DELIVERANCE

"I cannot carry all these people by myself; the burden is too heavy for me." V14

It is essential for every leader to embrace this spiritual reality. Only God can truly carry our burdens. **We are not created to carry things in our own strength; it is only in God's strength and grace that we are enabled to be spiritual burden-bearers. As leaders we are simply entrusted with grace for stewardship of those responsibilities within our God-given spheres of influence.**

Jesus said, *"Come to me all you who are weary and burdened and I will give you rest ..."* Matthew 11:28 (-30)

Whilst the Lord's words are intended to comfort all believers, this Scripture becomes especially poignant in their context of ministry to the heart of a burdened leader. Jesus is the One who give us the gift of supernatural rest especially during challenging leadership situations. We are simply required to enter this rest by faith.

APOSTOLIC LEADERSHIP INTERVENTION = GAP STANDING

IDENTIFY TEAM, DESIGNATE ROLES, DELEGATE RESPONSIBILITIES

"The Lord said to Moses, Bring me seventy of Israel's elders who are known to you as leaders and officials among the people. Have them come to the Tent of Meeting that they may stand there with you. I will come down and speak to you there, and I will take of the Spirit that is on you and put the Spirit on them. They will help you carry the burden of the people so that you will not have to carry it alone." Numbers 11:16-17

God wanted to create an apostolic team and He instructed His servant Moses to gather a specific number of those whom Moses had already identified with leadership potential. It makes sense when one is thirsty, to draw from a well that is already dug; **the spiritual parallel for leadership is that when leadership is needed in a time of crisis, it is wisdom to recruit those who are already anointed and gifted in leadership**. There is most definitely a time for encouraging new leaders and those with leadership potential and equipping them for the next level; however, there are also seasons (particularly in mobilisation), when established key leaders are the most appropriate choice for that time.

APOSTOLIC MINISTRY IS A SHARED MINISTRY

Apostolic ministry is not meant to be an isolated ministry. It is a shared ministry. Jesus saw fit to set the apostolic ministry on twelve sets of shoulders. The apostles then ensured than another (Matthias) took the place of Judas after his suicide. *"Then they prayed, "Lord, you know everyone's heart. Show us which of these two you have chosen, to take over this apostolic ministry, which Judas left to go where he belongs." Then they cast lots, and the lot fell to Matthias; so he was added to the eleven apostles."* (Acts 1:24-26)

THE ANOINTING ENABLES US TO FULFILL OUR ASSIGNMENT

"I will come down and speak with you there, and I will take of the Spirit that is on you and put the Spirit on them. They will help you carry the burden of the people so that you will not have to carry it alone." (v17)

When the anointing came upon them there was prophecy in the camp (v26). But the leadership team were not given the Spirit just so that they could prophesy – they were given the Holy Spirit to help them lead! The Holy Spirit enables us to fulfil our assignments. Moses was able to identify, inspire and appoint a core team to help him lead. As leaders we have to learn to appoint, anoint and authorise delegated representatives as well as designate particular roles and responsibilities to capable individuals.

We can learn from the blueprint God gave to Moses that an effective leader must learn:

How to identify problems/issues

- Bring those burdens and issues to God in a prayerful manner
- Rely entirely on God's grace to bring deliverance
- Recognise and receive the God-given blue print for managing issues
- Co-operate and apply the divinely-mandated solution given by God - in this case appoint those with proven leadership experience
- Appoint apostolic teams in designated roles with delegated authority/spheres of influence
- Ensure all those appointed to be part of the apostolic team leadership are anointed by the Holy Spirit.

PROVISION FROM GOD VIS A VIS THE 'GRAVE OF CRAVINGS'

The people of God had been instructed to consecrate themselves (v18) in preparation for the Lord's provision for their "cravings." The provision came in the form of a wind that blew in a multitude of quail from the sea to the land. The

Israelites were able to gather a phenomenal amount of food, but the Lord's anger burned against them and he struck some with a severe plague. The place was called *Kibroth Hattaavah*, which means "*grave of cravings.*" It serves as a sombre reminder to us not to despise the Lord's provision. Unrestrained, the cravings of our flesh will only lead to spiritual death.

Apostle Peter exhorted believers to, "*rid yourselves of all malice and all deceit, hypocrisy, envy, and slander of every kind. Like newborn babies, crave pure spiritual milk, so that by it you may grow up in your salvation, now that you have tasted that the Lord is good.*" 1 Peter 2:2

To crave means, v. *1. Feel a powerful desire for.* God spoke to the Israelites that they were to consecrate themselves in order to receive His provision to meet their cravings. It is only by our being one with Christ that we are consecrated i.e. made sacred.

God longs for us to surrender to His perfect and holy desires for our lives. When we surrender to Him in this manner, His righteousness becomes a plumb-line upon which we can relate, respond and grow up into mature sons and daughters; we please God with our faith here on earth and by living lives that reflect Christ-likeness.

God only wants the best for us and wants to fill us to overflowing with every good thing. Jesus said, *"Blessed are those who hunger and thirst for righteousness, for they will be filled." Matthew 5:6*

I ask you to pause for a moment today and think on the things that you most desire in life. If Jesus isn't as the top of your list, spend some time reflecting on that and ask God to order your life according to His priorities for you. If you know in your heart and mind that you have a craving for something that is contrary to the will of God ask God's forgiveness and receive a fresh infilling of the Holy Spirit to cleanse and empower you to walk in obedience to God's will. Holy Spirit is a wonderful teacher and helps to guide our feet to walk in paths of righteousness.

"Therefore, prepare your minds for action; be self-controlled; set your hope fully on the grace to be given you when Jesus Christ is revealed." 1 Peter 1:13

MOBILISATION AND MANAGEMENT

- A STUDY IN THE LIFE OF MOSES

CHAPTER 4: COMPROMISE IN THE HOUSE

MOSES' LEADERSHIP ATTACKED

Miriam and Aaron began to talk against Moses because of his Cushite wife, for he had married a Cushite. "Has the LORD spoken only through Moses?" they asked. "Hasn't he also spoken through us?" And the LORD heard this." Numbers 12:1-2

Every Godly leader will most likely experience some kind of 'attack' against their ministry at some point and often from those who are closest to them in ministry (or from family members). In the case our study of Moses, it was the latter situation that presented, when his sister Miriam and brother Aaron spoke out against him.

It was said of Moses, *"Now Moses was a very humble man, more humble than anyone on the face of the earth)"* Numbers 12:3

Leaders endure much persecution in their calling, but they also receive grace to walk in the beautiful humble nature of Christ. Humility is a key to overcoming the potentially disabling effects of personal attack upon one's leadership, because in humility one is hidden in the character and integrity of Christ, dependent upon His grace and reliant upon release of His wisdom and compassion into difficult situations to bring about healing and reconciliation.

To compromise means: to bring into disrepute or danger by indiscreet or reckless behaviour. Miriam and Aaron were being disrespectful about Moses and speaking out against his apostolic/prophetic calling. Miriam's words veer towards envy and jealousy – perhaps not only of Moses' calling, but also with respect to the holy intimacy that he enjoyed with the Lord. As we will see from the following Scriptures, the consequence of Miriam's words against her brother was devastating and certainly posed a serious danger to her God-given destiny.

Sadly, not only was there compromise in God's house, but Miriam's words reflect that there was also condescension in Miriam's heart. **To condescend means to show that one feels superior to.** Miriam and Aaron expressed superiority against Moses in relation to the prophetic revelations they felt they had received from God. They lacked humility and understanding about the calling on Moses' life. Their words reflect their lack of understanding and spiritual immaturity.

God does not ignore compromise in His house. Indeed, the Scripture reveals that He deals with it in righteousness and does so speedily and with open dialogue.

"At once the LORD said to Moses, Aaron and Miriam, "Come out to the Tent of Meeting all three of you." So the three of them came out. Then the LORD came down in a pillar of cloud; he stood at the entrance to the tent, and summoned Aaron and Miriam. When both of them stepped forward, he said, "Listen to my words," Numbers 12:4-6

God Confirms Moses as an Apostolic Leader

"When a prophet of the LORD is among you, I reveal myself to him in visions, I speak to him in dreams. But this is not true of my servant Moses; he is faithful in all my house. With him I speak face to face, clearly and not in riddles; he sees the form of the LORD. Why then were you not afraid to speak against my servant Moses?" Numbers 12:6-8

Miriam and Aaron would have had no doubt at this point that God was Moses' advocate and that He graciously affirmed the apostolic/prophetic leadership mantle upon his servant's life. God affirmed his humble servant and then addressed the issue of speaking against Moses. Humility before God will always result in God championing His beloved ones when under any kind of spiritual onslaught.

Be blessed this day dear friends as you meditate on God's word and to all who are hurting I pray for healing in the mighty name of Jesus.

MOBILISATION AND MANAGEMENT

- A STUDY IN THE LIFE OF MOSES

CHAPTER 5: CROSSING INTO DESTINY

In following Moses we can clearly see that God is always interested in each one of our heart's condition, and He uses the crucible of leadership challenges to hone our characters and cause us to become more like Him. Allow me to share an experience with you from the time when I was leading a global praise initiative, "One Million Hours of Praise":

Vision Killers

It's been my experience that every visionary will encounter 'vision killers' and that God uses such 'vision killers' to test our commitment, our character and prove our faith. A vision killer is someone who will criticise, judge and/or condemn vision or the visionary in a forthright and sometimes aggressive manner.   Vision killers can either be sent by God or the enemy. I discovered this anonymous quote the other day and thought it succinctly (if somewhat wryly) summed up the point. "*A successful person is one who can lay a firm foundation with the bricks that others throw at them.*"

During the preparation stage of One Million Hours of Praise, God allowed a particular "vision killer" to contact me. This gentleman called me on the phone one evening and said he had been praying for me and he felt that I was not the one to lead One Million Hours of Praise. He went on to say that in his opinion the vision was not a Godly vision. I quietly listened to him and then responded with humility and faith. I said I would take his concerns to my Council of Advisors and share with them. I was willing to do whatever they felt was right. I thanked him for sharing what he thought was God's will but I reminded him that I had not sought his counsel or input. Secondly, I corrected the brother by reminding him that we were made to praise the Lord and that we will spend eternity praising Jesus, so although I was willing to consider God might call someone else to lead the vision, I was not willing to concede that praise is an ungodly activity.

I reported back to each one of my Council of Advisors and each of them thought I ought to continue and affirmed my role as lead facilitator. God had permitted the 'vision killer' to test my commitment to the Million Hours of Praise vision and was also testing my character to see if I was able to remain a woman of righteous integrity under "rapid enemy fire!"

Building and Finishing

Many people are good at starting but they do not finish. In outworking vision there is much hard work, trials and testing that lie ahead. God will allow vision to appear to die so that He can resurrect it for His glory. Every vision/visionary must journey to and through the Cross. I have quickly learned that if I haven't given the vision back to God, God cannot sustain the vision. We have to come to the end of ourselves and our own resources so that we can fully step into God miracle provision. Ultimately, God will let only let us move forward when He is convinced of our commitment."

(Extract from Catherine Brown's book, "Kingdom Building – Realising Vision and Developing Leaders")

Despite the comments from the vision killer, God graced me to lead and facilitate the kingdom initiative, *One Million Hours of Praise*, which raised more than a millions hours of praise, with a global day of praise, partners in more than 60 nations and countless testimonies of salvations, healings and Holy Spirit baptisms.

Compromise against other Leaders is like Leprosy

"The anger of the LORD burned against them, and he left them. When the cloud lifted from above the Tent, there stood Miriam – leprous, like snow. Aaron turned toward her and saw that she had leprosy; and he said to Moses, "Please my lord, do not hold against us the sin we have so foolishly committed. Do not let her be like a

stillborn infant coming from its mother's womb with its flesh half eaten away." Numbers 12:9-12

Because of her sin, Miriam was struck with leprosy by God and her skin turned white like snow. Miriam could be considered a leader in her own right, yet she was suffering for her sin of compromise towards her brother. Her reckless words almost cost her destiny and show us that an ungodly attitude towards others in leadership has the potential to adversely affect our God-given calling.

It is essential that we honour one another and operate in mutual respect as leaders with respect to other leaders and also as those under authority to leadership. Our attitude towards leadership is a reflection of our ability to submit to God's authority. I have found that some people have been damaged by abuse of authority in life and/or in ministry situations and this is the reason why they may struggle to submit to Godly authority. True Christ-like authority is given to build others up and not knock people down. As leaders we are able to administer healing to those who have been abused by the wrong use of authority, so that they might see the true reflection of Christ through us. Regardless of our life experiences, we are all required to submit to Christ and His rulership over our lives as our personal Lord and Saviour.

Miriam's experience shows us clearly that our compromise is not hidden before God and that it can have serious consequences. Paul teaches us to model unity in the body of Christ and in this way blessings will flow amongst God's people as we move in the bond of peace.

"Be completely humble and gentle; be patient, bearing with one another in love. Make every effort to keep the unity of the Spirit through the bond of peace." Ephesians 4:2-3

APOSTOLIC LEADERSHIP INTERVENTION = GAP STANDING IN PRAYER

Moses' response to his sister's betrayal was to cry out to the Lord,
"O God, please heal her." Numbers 12:13

Moses' response, must also be the heart cry of every leader, no matter how hurt or betrayed they may feel. The Godly leader must learn to stand in the gap no matter what and call down the mercy of God to bring restoration to people who have sinned. Jesus reached out to the leper and healed him. God is always willing and able to heal an earnest, confessing heart. Glory to His name!

MOBILISATION AND MANAGEMENT

- A STUDY IN THE LIFE OF MOSES

CHAPTER 6: OVERCOMING OFFENCE

In closing our study of this chapter of Moses' life with respect to leading and mobilising the body of Christ, I would like to share some further insights from my book, *"Kingdom Building – Realising Vision and Developing Leaders."*

Understand the Pitfalls

Relationships have layers of blessings and challenges. Determine to love people no matter what and be tenacious in holding on to God-given relationships.

- Choose and determine to relate to people you work with or every small hurdle will offend you
- Overcome small problems by focusing on grace to reach a higher goal together
- Don't work from the negative or from the past
- Understand there will be mountain tops and valleys i.e. highs and lows, lovely times and difficult times.
- Leadership has lonely phases; it is normal and is part of apostolic identification with Christ

Don't Operate in Offence

"Only in his hometown, among his relatives and in his own house is a prophet without honour." Mark 6:3

People generally will not be as committed as you [the leader] and will come up with lots of excuses but keep on loving and (when necessary) don't be afraid to discipline. Godly discipline is part of being a disciple. Some people will deny you and walk away after committing to you; sometimes God will allow you to see this coming but at other times not. Remember He is interested in developing your character too.

People sometimes walk away because they are in need of personal healing. Jesus spent time with the outcasts of society – demoniacs, lepers, paralytics, prostitutes, tax collectors and dead people to name a few. Critically, Jesus was willing and able to see beyond their circumstances and speak to the potential He saw in them, reaching out to heal them when necessary and working with them in partnership for God's glory.

Some people will betray you but purpose to keep on loving, forgive others, maintain relationships with them where possible and move on. Dealing with personal betrayal has been one of my deepest lessons learned as a leader but I am grateful for the process that led me into a place of greater understanding of Christ's agape.

Jesus was once approached by a leper who said, *"Lord if you are willing you can make me clean."* Jesus reached out His hand and touched the man and said, *"I am willing"* and immediately the man was made clean and healed of his leprosy. Offence is a type of spiritual leprosy. Don't let it get a foothold. If you do not operate in offence, you will then have the authority and compassion to deliver others. Model acceptance and forgiveness and you will create a Christ-centred environment for growth and personal development.

Perhaps the most significant way in which we can remain people orientated and develop our Kingdom relationships is to emulate Jesus in obeying His Father thus, *"For I did not speak on my own accord, but the Father who sent me commanded me what to say and how to say it. I know that his command leads to eternal life. So whatever I say is just what the Father has told me to say." John 12:49-50*

(**Extract from Catherine Brown's book** *"Kingdom Building – Realising Vision and Developing Leaders"*)

How can a leader become more people-orientated?

It would seem somewhat of a paradox to suggest that a leader needs to become more people orientated when leading itself is a people-focused task! However, once you have spent a lot of time around people, there are moments when you simply need to close the door and be as far away from the 'madding crowd' as possible.

On the other hand, here are just a few simple suggestions on how we can become more people-orientated.

By aspiring to be a motivational manager and being intentional about caring for others we can foster and develop relationships.

- An essential aspect of being a motivational manager is to model what you desire to multiply in others. Jesus taught ministry, then modelled ministry allowing His disciples to learn with Him and then He let them do it by themselves once they were competent.

- A motivational manager is not just concerned about training people for task, but is also interested and committed to developing leadership potential in others. It's about what we can give to others, not what we can take from them.

- Jesus **loved** His disciples; if we don't have God's love as one of our core foundational values we will become easily corrupted.

- Jesus **prayed** for His disciples; pray for your partners/team. Your prayers will enable them to have faith to aspire to greater things (*John 14:12*)

Yours in the love of our King
Catherine Brown

ABOUT THE AUTHOR

Catherine Brown is the Apostolic Founder/Director of Gatekeepers Global Ministries (GGM), and the co-founder of the Scottish Apostolic Networking Enterprise. She is a sought-after international preacher and teacher. She is presently leading a global apostolic evangelism and discipleship mission entitled, "GGM 7 Million Souls" and is working with her team and valued partners from many nations in evangelism, discipleship, church planting and on-going support and development of pastors/leaders. By God's grace, GGM ministry and partners have seen almost 50,000 conversions with 82 church plants. GGM also has a developing network of leaders who affiliate with GGM ministry vision and values.

Catherine is married to Stephen and they have four lovely children and live on the West coast of Scotland. She has authored many books, teachings and pamphlets.

Gatekeepers Global Ministries

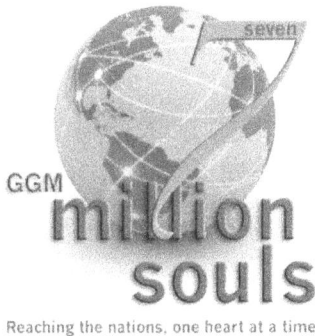

GGM

million
souls

Reaching the nations, one heart at a time

www.gatekeepers.org.uk
admin@gatekeepers.org.uk

OTHER BOOKS BY CATHERINE BROWN

(All available worldwide via Amazon)

Simply Apostolic (3 Volume Set)

"Simply Apostolic" is an eye-opener into the often controversial world of apostolic ministry. Catherine Brown has written fearlessly and comprehensively on the topic of authentic apostolic ministry, bringing cutting edge insight into the gift and function of apostles and apostolic ministry in the 21st century church.

Respected senior Christian leaders from around the world have endorsed this daring and controversial book. Throughout, it clearly outlines valuable authentic Kingdom principles and practical protocols on apostolic functionality, and takes the reader on an amazing behind-the-scenes journey to understand what it means to be a "sent one".

This book is a profound combination of courageous articulation of biblical truth, sound doctrine, wisdom and practical experience written in a clear, concise, practical and unpretentious style.

For those interested in advancing the Kingdom of God and understanding more about apostolic leadership, this volume will deliver priceless knowledge and insight.

Paperback ISBN's
Volume 1 - 9781909805064
Volume 2 – 9781909805040
Volume 3 – 9781909805095

eBook ISBN's
Volume 1 - 9781909805101
Volume 2 – 9781909805118
Volume 3 - 9781909805125

Kingdom Building –
Realising Vision and Developing Leaders

This book seeks to envision emerging leaders and also equips existing leaders to step out in bold Kingdom ventures.

Catherine's latest book is a must read for all established visionary leaders and for those who are emerging as aspiring leaders. It is full of wisdom and solid biblical teaching. Catherine draws from her own ministry experience in leading global vision and does so in a transparent and straightforward fashion. The topics in the books include how to recognise your season in the Lord, how to conceive, consolidate and build foundations for vision. How to be prepared to carry vision, how to implement, share and lead vision to completion. Advice on partnership, vision, values, balance in leadership, investing in team, setting goals, dealing with enemy opposition and obtaining counter strategy and much, much more.

"This is a wonderfully practical book that melds together Godly values with our best efforts to bring forth Kingdom strategy. It challenges us to lay a true foundation for realizing vision by nurturing the right heart attitude with God and our fellow ministry partners. Then it builds on that solid foundation with straightforward and accessible principles and guidelines. May visions be realized; May leaders be developed; May God's Kingdom Come."

Rev. Wesley Zinn, Wellspring Church

ISBN's
Paperback 9781909805149
ebook 9781909805071

ENCOUNTER – LESSONS IN CHRISTIAN LEADERSHIP (VOLUMES 1-3)

The "*Encounter – Lessons in Christian Leadership*" series written by Catherine Brown is a succession of life study booklets on some of the great leaders of both the Old Testament and the New Testament, which focus on Kingdom leadership principles and practical applications of spiritual truths. In addition to sound Scriptural teaching, Catherine also shares from her own extensive personal experience as a Christian leader. Over the last 15 years she has worked alongside many churches and ministries in varying capacities including overseeing churches and ministries; developing and outworking strategy/vision at local, national and international levels for prayer, worship, evangelism, church planting and discipleship as well as leadership development in church and conference settings and in the market place. This series has already received excellent feedback from Church leaders, who have been encouraged and strengthened through reading.

The first volume in the series, "*Mobilisation and Management – A Study in the Life of Moses*" is a succinct creative analysis in the life of an inspirational leader of the Christian faith: Moses, a servant leader with a Kingdom mission and mind set.

Volume two of the Encounter series focuses on the life and trials of Joseph as an apostolic leader for the nation of Israel.

Paperback ISBN's
Volume 1 - 9781909805194
Volume 2 – 9781909805200

eBook ISBN's
Volume 1 - 9780956208668
Volume 2 – 9781909805118

TO ISRAEL WITH LOVE

The message in **To Israel with Love** will help the reader break free from hatred, indifference and ignorance as they discover the eternal truth about God's love and covenant with the Jewish people.

"Catherine has truly captured the Father's heart for Israel and the Jewish people through a mother's eyes. The prophetic insight is as new wine for a new day!"

Curt Landry, House of David Ministries

Catherine Brown has written a book laced with prophetic spirit. She interweaves prophetic visions, solid Scriptural exposition and words directly from King Abba's heart. The resulting balance is simultaneously alive, encouraging and refreshing.

Catherine, like Ruth of old, has found rest and prophetic refreshment under the shade of Israel's olive tree, and the blessing on her words is proof positive of her blessing of Israel.

The prophetic sap of God's ancient olive tree runs through this book. Enjoy!"

Avner Boskey, David's Tent www.davidstent.org

Currently only available as an eBook

ISBN
ebook 9780956208651

MIRACLES AND MAYHEM –
THE MINISTRY OF FAMILIES

Miracles and Mayhem charts God's heart for families and the biblical foundation for family life and is a compelling account of a family's every day journey together in the Kingdom of God.

"Don't buy this book if you want a God that is safe, predictable and cosily locked up in a box only to be opened on Sundays. Don't buy this book if you want to feel safe in your daily life from a God who invades the ordinary and makes it extraordinary. However, do buy it if you long for the reality of a God who can come into the chaos of family life and speak to you through ordinary everyday incidents. If you want a God who talks to ordinary people and shows them extraordinary things and uses them to touch a hurting world with healing grace, then do buy this book. You won't regret it."

Rev Eric Delve, Chairman of Revival Fire Conferences

"Catherine's book is heart-warming. You will be challenged, touched and encouraged as you read about her family. You will be blessed as you enjoy Catherine and Stephen's journey, and spiritual insight."

Dr. Heidi Baker, Director Iris Ministries

ISBN's
Paperback 9788190249164
ebook 9780956208620

CONFESSIONS OF A FASTING HOUSEWIFE (ONE WOMAN'S JOURNEY WITH JESUS)

Confessions of a Fasting Housewife is an open and honest diary of Catherine's attempt to fast for 40 days and serves as a guide to anyone considering a fast whether short or extended. This book is described as, "*more than a spiritual guide to fasting - it is a practical primer on the "dos and don'ts" of fasting.* As you read Catherine Brown's experiences, you will find yourself empathising, and at times, outright laughing at her candid confessions of the emotional ups and downs involved with fasting in the 21st century. Spirituality and practicality meet head-on in *Confessions of a Fasting Housewife*. Get ready to learn everything your pastor never told you about fasting! Then ... fast!

Victoria Boyson writer of the foreword states, "*Confessions of a Fasting Housewife is a masterpiece of mercy and will open up your heart and mind to receive the grace to love God more than ever.*"

Currently only available as a paperback

ISBN
Paperback 9788889127100

THE NORMAL, THE DEEP AND THE CRAZY
(Catherine's Testimony)

Available in English, French and Spanish

The Normal, the Deep and the Crazy, is a transparent and moving account of Catherine's life with a violent and alcoholic father, her illegitimacy and her healing testimony since she found the Lord. The book is written in an amazingly transparent style and has been described as "*A light for your journey, a hope for your heart and a mission for your life.*"

James Goll writer of the foreword says, "*With a whole heart I gladly endorse the contents of this inspiring book. I trust it will do for you, what it did for me. I found myself more in love with our Father God who desires to see restoration happen in the lives of countless warriors-in-waiting.*"

Paperback ISBN's
English - 9780956208606
French - 9782952367097

eBook ISBN's
English - 9781909805002
Spanish - 9780956208613

THE STORY OF LEAH
(OVERCOMING REJECTION)

The courage and tenacity of Leah in the midst of extremely difficult circumstances have spoken profoundly to Catherine on overcoming rejection. This short volume will inspire and delight the reader as the author comprehensively addresses the issues surrounding rejection by winding her own personal experiences through the rich biblical tapestry of the story of Leah.

ISBN's
Paperback 9781909805293
ebook 9781909805286

LOVE YOUR NEIGHBOUR –
COMMUNITY TRANSFORMATION

A basic discipleship manual which is available free of charge to all registered Gatekeepers Global Ministries partners.